THANK YOU GOD

Published by Tughra Books
345 Clifton Ave., Clifton,
NJ, 07011, USA

www.tughrabooks.com

Project Editor: Betül Ertekin
Copy Editors: Eyüp Aygün, Amrozia Tabssam
Illustrations: Süleyman Özkonuk
Graphic Design: İbrahim Akdağ

ISBN: 978-1-59784-235-8

Printed by
Çağlayan A.Ş. Izmir, Turkey

Dear mothers, fathers and other educators,

"Thank You God" is designed to help our children learn about the beauties that surround them and to help them feel God's love. Along with reading the prayers in this book, the tasks in the Coloring and Activity Book should be done. In this way your children will not only get to know their environment better, but they will also experience the joy of thanking God.

Thank You God, for letting me come to this world.

I am happy to be able to see everything and to be able to hear, taste, and touch.

Help me God to be a healthy person and a person who You will love.

God, please give me, and those whom I love a long life.

Thank You God, for giving me such a lovely mother.

My mother makes me delicious food.

She is always with me whenever I am sick.

I feel safe when she hugs me.

I love her smell.

God please let my mother always be with me.

Thank You God, for giving me a strong and hard-working father.

He usually comes home from work late and tired, but he still has time for me.

I love him so much; sometimes I surprise him.

Please let him always be with me.

God, give my father strength.

Thank You God, for my cute baby sister.

I thought that my mother and father would stop loving me when she was born; I was mistaken.

My sister's nose is exactly like mine.

When I play games with her, I am very happy.

God, I want to be with my sister all the time.

I never want to be separated from her.

Thank You God, for my grandma and grandpa.

I love it when they put me on their lap and hug me.

I love my grandparents very much.

I feel bad when they are sick.

God, give my grandmother and grandfather a healthy long life.

Thank You God, for giving my family and I a home to share.

I love our home and my room.

Our house is very warm.

And we have everything we need in it.

I feel safe at home.

God, please help out children who don't have a house.

Give them a warm home to live in.

Thank You God, for giving me my own room.

I have my own bed, cupboard, desk and toys; in fact, I have everything in my room.

Now that I am older I can tidy up my room by myself.

This makes my mother and father very happy.

God, please help me keep my room tidy.

Thank You God, for giving me my own bed.

I feel so comfortable when I am sleeping in my bed.

Sometimes I have scary dreams at night.

My mother says that if I say 'Bismillah' before I go to sleep, I won't be afraid.

From now on I am going to sleep on my right side.

I heard this from my grandfather.

Our Prophet always did this, too.

God, help me have pleasant dreams in my sleep.

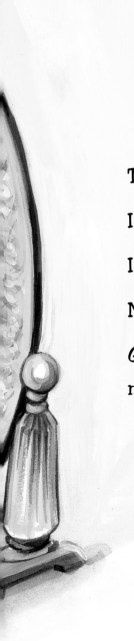

Thank You God, for my clothes.

I feel very comfortable when I wear them.

I look very nice when I wear them.

Now I can choose what to wear myself.

God, help me to always choose pretty clothes which fit me perfectly.

Thank You God, for all my toys.

I have so much fun when I play with them.

I am so happy when I share them with my friends.

And I always remember to put them away when I have finished playing.

Thank You God, for giving me such nice toys.

Thank You God, for all the books I have.

I love to look at the pictures, do the activities, and listen to the stories in them.

Please! God, let me have more books and help me to be a knowledgeable person.

26

Thank You God, for all the colorful crayons that I have.

I can make really beautiful pictures with my crayons.

I give them as gifts to people I love.

I love You very much for giving me these.

Thank You God, for all the sweets, chocolate, fruit and vegetables that I eat.

They all taste delicious and their shapes and colors are so beautiful.

I know that You have made all the food so that we can have a healthy life and I love You very much for this.

29

Thank You God, for my beautiful school.

I love to go to school and see my teacher and my friends.

I learn something new every day.

I sing songs, and recite poems and say tongue twisters.

Please help me God do well at school.

Thank You God, for my loving, kind-hearted teacher.

I love it when she tells me "Well done."

I know that she loves me very much.

Dear God, I wish my teacher could always be with me.

Thank You God, for my wonderful friends.

I love to play games with them and do different things.

Dear God, help me to be a good friend to them.

Thank You God, for making me a good child.

I love everything that You have created, Dear God.

I water the plants in my home.

I feed the hungry cats in the street.

I share everything with my friends.

I help the elderly.

My mother says that You love me even more when I do these.

She says good people go to Heaven.

Dear God, help me be a good person all my life.

Thank You God, for sending Prophet Muhammad (pbuh) who was full of love.

My mother says that his face had a heavenly light.

Also that he had a beautiful scent like roses.

Prophet Muhammad (pbuh) loved children very much.

I wish he could have loved me, too.

My mother tells me that I will be able to see our Prophet (pbuh) in Heaven.

Dear God I love our Prophet Muhammad (pbuh) and all the other prophets very much; please let them love me as well.

Thank You God, for the beautiful country I live in.

I love it very much.

I love the seas, the trees, the flowers, and the beautiful green countryside.

My father told me that many kinds of fruits and vegetables are grown in our country.

He told me that there are many countries in the world, all with different beautiful things.

Dear God, help me see all these beautiful places when I grow up.

Help me have a happy life in my country.

Thank You God, for loving me and my family.

Also, for creating my body in such a beautiful shape.

Thank You, for giving me intelligence, for making me caring and helpful, and for the colorful and beautiful scented flowers.

Thank You very much.

Thank You, for the green trees and grass, for the flying birds, butterflies and insects, for the dogs, cats, rabbits and turtles, for the sun that heats and gives us light.

Thank You God, for the moon and the shining stars that light up the night sky, for the fish and starfish that swim in the sea, for the water we drink and wash ourselves with.

Thank You, for all these beautiful things that You have created.

Thank You God, as much as the number of the leaves of the trees and the waves of the seas, drops of the rain, and the snow flakes.

GOD, I LOVE YOU SO MUCH...

SONG
ALHAMDULILLAH

Thinking, walking people
The fish that swim in the sea
The tiny insects
For these I say Alhamdulillah
For these I say Alhamdulillah

The trees, the flowers, the grass
The flying birds and butterflies
The tiny insects
For these I say Alhamdulillah
For these I say Alhamdulillah

The dogs, the cats, the rabbits
The flying birds and butterflies
The tiny insects
For these I say Alhamdulillah
For these I say Alhamdulillah